ONE OF US

ONE OF US

by Robin Chapman

LONDON

A member of the Chappell and Intersong Music Group

First published 1986 by
ETG, English Theatre Guild Ltd,
129 Park Street, London W1Y 3FA.

© Copyright Robin Chapman 1986

ISBN 0 85676 131 1

Typeset and printed by Commercial Colour Press, London E7.
Cover design by Robin Lowry.

'One must be fond of people and trust them if one is not to make a mess of one's life, and it is therefore essential that they should not let one down. They often do. Personal relations are despised today. They are regarded as bourgeois luxuries, as products of a time of fair weather which is now past, and we are urged to get rid of them, and to dedicate ourselves to some movement or cause instead. I hate the idea of causes, and if I had to choose between betraying my country and betraying my friend, I hope I should have the guts to betray my country. Such a choice may scandalise the modern reader, and he may stretch out his patriotic hand to the telephone and ring up the police. It would not have shocked Dante, however. Dante placed Brutus and Cassius in the lowest circle of Hell because they had chosen to betray their friend Julius Caesar rather than their country Rome ... '

E M Forster
TWO CHEERS FOR DEMOCRACY
Edward Arnold (Publishers) Ltd

ONE OF US was first presented at Greenwich Theatre, London, on 12 February 1986, with the following cast:

REES	Anthony Andrews
GUY	Ian Ogilvy
MARGIE	Jenny Quayle
ANTHONY	David Horovitch

Directed by Alan Strachan
Designed by Bob Crowley
Lighting by John A. Williams

The play takes place in the garden of Rees's home at Sonning-on-Thames. Early summer 1951.

Act I

Sunday, 6th May. Early evening.

ACT II

| Scene 1 | Sunday, 27th May. Night. |
| Scene 2 | Monday, 28th May. Morning. |

CHARACTERS

GORONWY REES
GUY BURGESS
MARGIE REES
ANTHONY BLUNT

NOTE:

GORONWY REES born 1909, educated at Cardiff Grammar
School and New College, Oxford. Journalist, author and
translator. Volunteered for military service in 1939, first with
the Royal Artillery then with the Royal Welch Fusiliers and as
a staff officer to General Montgomery rising to the rank of
Lt.-Colonel. After the war Rees continued as a freelance author
and was appointed Estates Bursar to All Souls College, Oxford.
Later he became Principal of the University of Wales at
Aberystwyth. He died in 1979.

GUY BURGESS born 1911, educated Dartmouth Naval College,
Eton and Trinity College, Cambridge. BBC talks producer and
minor diplomat. Joined MI6 in 1939. Later PPS to Hector
McNeil, Minister of State for Foreign Affairs in the post-war
Labour administration. Posted to the British Embassy in
Washington in 1950; he defected to Russia with Donald
Maclean in 1951. (Their presence was not however officially
acknowledged until 1956). Burgess died in Moscow in 1963.

MARGIE REES born 1922, married Goronwy Rees in 1941; they
had five children. She died in 1976.

ANTHONY BLUNT born in 1907, educated at Marlborough and
Trinity College, Cambridge. Art historian. Director of the
Courtauld Institute and Surveyor of the King's then the
Queen's pictures. Served in MI5 during the war. Knighted in
1956, Blunt was secretly granted immunity from prosecution by
MI5 in 1964 but was publicly exposed as a traitor in 1979. He
died in 1983.

In 1951, Goronwy Rees was forty-two, Guy Burgess forty,
Margie Rees twenty-nine and Anthony Blunt forty-four.

PREFACE

One Of Us is an historical play and as such is, of course, a work
of the imagination based upon fact. By this I mean that the
reader or spectator may rest assured that the four characters
represented did exist, that the meetings between them actually
took place, that other events and persons referred to in the text
were equally real and that Goronwy Rees's final decision to
inform MI5 of what he knew was followed through by him—if
not by anyone else. The hypothesis from which the action of the
play evolves—that Guy Burgess was recalled from the United
States by Anthony Blunt—is my own imaginative but
reasonable assumption drawn from the historical facts as they
are presently known. Everything else is fiction.

Robin Chapman
August, 1986

photograph by Stephen Moreton Prichard from the Greenwich Theatre production of One Of Us

ACT ONE

Sunday, 6th May. Evening sunlight on the garden. REES *sits in a wicker chair reading a Foreign Office memorandum with concentration. Two other chairs, low table with a bottle of Bells' whisky, soda siphon and tumblers. A scatter of children's previously loved toys.* REES *sips his whisky as he turns a page then, puzzled, turns back to check an earlier paragraph. He sighs.*

REES   Oh, really.

                (*He reads on again, tugging at his ear, a characteristic
                gesture. Clearly he is not impressed with the contents of
                this buff folder enclosing closely-typed, sky-blue foolscap.
                Inside the house the phone rings three times before it is
                answered. Pause.*)

MARGIE   (*off, calling*) Rees darling, phone. Phone, darling.
                Rees. Rees. Phone.

REES   Who? Who is it?

MARGIE   (*off*) Oxford. All Souls.

REES   (*rising*) Blast.

                (*He folds the memo back hard to keep the page he is at,
                leaves it on his chair. Exit* REES. *Pause. Enter* GUY
                *from the garden. He looks round, lights a Camel
                cigarette from a Zippo lighter then picks up the memo,
                unfolding it to check the page* REES *has reached.*)

GUY   Thirteen.

                (*Enter* MARGIE *with a bottle of Chablis and two wine
                glasses on a tray.*)

MARGIE   Rees is on the phone.

GUY   I heard it ring.

MARGIE   Oxford. All Souls.

GUY   That figures—as the Yankees say.

                (*Pause.*)

MARGIE   Rees said you'd like a glass of Chablis—with
                soda?

GUY   Did he?

MARGIE	Now you're off spirits.
GUY	Your other half seriously suggests I mix piss with wind?
MARGIE	That's what he said.
GUY	Good Lord—then the end of the world is well and truly nigh.
MARGIE	I know you prefer red wine really. Rees shouldn't be long.
	(*Pause.*)
GUY	Tell me, I've often wondered, meant to ask, do you always call your husband by his surname?
MARGIE	I suppose so—I've never thought about it.
GUY	Even in bed?
MARGIE	Well—it's well shorter than Goronwy—isn't it?
GUY	Less of a mouthful possibly?
MARGIE	Mm.
GUY	How quaint. One tends to think of surnames as a male preserve. No—no soda—just the froggy pee-pee.
	(MARGIE *gives* GUY *his glass of Chablis.*)
	Chin-chin. Ya-boo. Happy days.
MARGIE	Yes.
	(*They drink.*)
GUY	Mm. Disgustingly delicious. Mm.
MARGIE	Why've you come?
GUY	Odd question. Thought it was obvious. As an old friend. Bearing gifts. For you all. Especially the kiddywinks.
MARGIE	But so soon?
GUY	Really? How soon is soon? In your book?

MARGIE	Well, I thought you said at lunch you only docked at Southampton yesterday?
GUY	Quite so. I did. Yes. Mm. True.
MARGIE	Now you're here. It's awfully quick.
GUY	You think so?
MARGIE	I know you're fond of Rees.
GUY	My oldest friend—bar one.
MARGIE	He gets so wrought up when he knows you're coming.
GUY	You astonish me.
MARGIE	This time he was tenser than ever.
GUY	Can't think why. No need to be. (*Pause.* GUY *indicates his empty glass.* MARGIE *refills it.*) Superdoop. So—Oxford has rescued a favourite son yet again?
MARGIE	Mm?
GUY	Your spouse—who else? His new appointment. Estates Bursar to All Souls—gee whiz.
MARGIE	Oh, that? Yes. Yes.
GUY	It keeps the wolf from the door?
MARGIE	Yes. He grumbles, of course.
GUY	I'm sure. It interposes itself between him and the writing of his latest masterpiece I expect?
MARGIE	So he says.
GUY	Not quite the cushy number he hoped for at first?
MARGIE	No. You see the college owns tracts of land, all over the country, literally thousands of acres. And Rees has had to review all their holdings—
GUY	So I gather. He gives his first annual report on the twenty-fifth, I understand? Correct?

MARGIE	You know everything.
GUY	You sound surprised by All Souls wealth?
MARGIE	Do I ? Not especially. Should I be?
GUY	No—not at all. After all, where would Oxbridge be without extensive slums and glorious grouse moors?

(MARGIE *yawns*.)

MARGIE	Oh, sorry—I didn't mean—I have to get up rather early with the children. Is it to do with that man in that club?
GUY	What?
MARGIE	That you've come?
GUY	You've lost me now.
MARGIE	I thought it might be.
GUY	What man? What club?
REES	(*off, calling*) Margie—cook wants you. Margie love.
MARGIE	Coming.
GUY	What man?
MARGIE	Ask Rees. Oh, and you won't forget you promised the girls a bedtime story?
GUY	Got oodles of those.
MARGIE	But not anything too exciting. Or they'll never get to sleep.
GUY	Don't worry—I'll give them my abridged version of *Pride and Prejudice* with the dirty bits kept in.

(*Enter* REES.)

REES	God! Oxford politics—phouf—they make Byzantium look like Workers' Playtime.
MARGIE	Put your cardigan on, darling. It's getting chilly.

REES   Don't fuss, Margie. I'm fine.

MARGIE   You weren't saying that a week ago. (MARGIE
            starts to exit but stops.) What does cook want?

REES   You. Something arcane about the soufflé for
            supper.

MARGIE   But she knows perfectly well how to do them—
            she taught me. (*Exit* MARGIE.)

GUY   You've been unwell?

REES   Not really. Touch of flu. Margie hasn't made a
            song and dance about it, I hope?

GUY   No. Just a trifle mother-hennish. Wishes I
            weren't here.

REES   Nonsense—

GUY   Oh, yes. Not to mention something about some
            man in some club?

REES   Margie said that?

GUY   Yes. Runic of her, I thought?

REES   Hadn't realized it had made such an impression.

GUY   What was it?

REES   No. You.

GUY   Me?

REES   Mm. First, yes—you, Guy, you. Why have you
            come down here? Really?

GUY   Jeepers creepers! You're worse than Margie!
            Oh, dear heart, haven't I said? How many
            times? Apart from being devoted to you all and
            needing a dose of pure *Wind in the Willows* after
            the States, I want your opinion of that! This
            memo. Which means much to me—may even
            salvage my career. And you haven't even read it
            yet! Page thirteen! Oh, Goronwy bach, you used
            to be a fast reader, brace of Russian novels
            before breakfast—you're losing your grip, boyo!

REES   I was reading it for a second time, Guy.

GUY   Oh? Ah—then you must've skipped the first?

REES   Not a word.

GUY   Oh. In that case what do you think? Sound?
            Cogent?

REES   Codswallop.

GUY   No, no, seriously, sweetheart. Do say. Your
            thoughts—at least *en principe?* I don't deceive
            myself, do I? I do offer a timely warning?
            People over here have got to realize and fast—
            just how crazy American policy's become! After
            all, when a US general can advocate dropping
            the atom bomb on North Korea—

REES   Guy—MacArthur got the sack last month. That
            particular loony's no longer on the loose in
            Korea—

GUY   Whitewash! Their policy remains the same. Oh,
            yes, Rees, yes—make no mistake we're all going
            to get vaporized to kingdom come but does our
            revered ambassador to the United States listen?
            Even though it's his job to relay such info back
            home? No. Refused to consider my memo.

REES   Well, it wasn't your job, was it, to provide this
            kind of analysis?

GUY   He should've been grateful—my mind's as good
            as his—my history's better!

REES   Rubbish—you know better than anybody how
            the Foreign Office works. Made it your business
            to know. As third secretary you couldn't hope—

GUY   Second secretary!

REES   Unattached. Nobody wanted you in
            Washington. You didn't smell right, you said—

GUY   Right you are, have it your way. But you must
            agree it's still important for this country to get
            the full low down on just how hysterically anti-

	communist America's become not only in Asia but at home too—
REES	Yes, yes, of course!
GUY	But are you aware, Rees, do you realize, that nowadays, thanks to Senator knuckle-bum McCarthy, queers in the US are equated automatically with Commies?
REES	(*laughing*) Well, let's face it, Guy, that's been known to happen here too, wouldn't you say? Look at yourself and Anthony—among so many other celebrated Marxist queens.
GUY	Don't try to be camp, ducky, it doesn't suit you.
REES	Oh? I beg your pardon. Do I gather I'm still not to mention Anthony by name? Even now? After all these years?
GUY	In a social context by all means but not—as you know—in a socialist one.
REES	He's a living paradox—I agree.
GUY	Aren't we all? (*Pause.*) Perhaps you'd better finish re-reading my memo so my visit won't have been entirely wasted—?
REES	No! Oh, no. Guy! That won't do! No! This can't be the reason—it's a smokescreen. Has to be!
GUY	For what?
REES	I'm asking you!
GUY	I want your view—honest Injun, cross my heart.
REES	You haven't got one!
GUY	Hope to die. I value your judgement, pickle.
	(*Pause.*)
REES	You're brazen. Utterly brazen.
GUY	My speciality.

REES	Well, since you insist—I think it's over-heated. And ill-balanced.
GUY	Ta ever so, sir, she said.
REES	My pleasure. Now. Tell me true. Why are you here?
GUY	You're all of a lather—my dear—
REES	No. Come on, Guy. Out with it. You hate Sonning-on-Thames—you warned me against taking this house—just as you warned me against marrying.
GUY	So I did. Fancy you remembering. Quite right. Yes, it's a bestial thought but it's more than likely I was actually begotten, shudderingly conceived at the White Hart. My parents honeymooned directly above the saloon bar. Legend has it such were the concommitant vibrations dry martinis mixed themselves. Can you wonder I warned you agin such friggery? Hey, Rees, did I ever tell you how Daddy actually died on the nest? And I had to pull Mummy out from under? That was later, of course, when I was thirteen.
REES	Yes, bi-annually I'd say you tell me on average, yes. Mm. Come along.
GUY	One's traumas are one's traumas.
	(*Pause.*)
REES	Yes?
	(*Pause.*)
GUY	Issues from the hand of God the simple soul.
	(*Pause.*)
REES	You're not usually at a loss for words, Guy.
GUY	Some things are difficult to put actually.
REES	Really? Very well. Perhaps it would help if I put your visit from my point of view?

GUY   If you like. You're the host.

REES   Well, to begin with, I get a rather excited letter
        from you in Washington saying you're being
        sent home for speeding through the State of
        Virginia.

GUY   Well, who wouldn't, poppet?

REES   Although in fact it wasn't you who'd committed
        this traffic offence but some boy you'd picked
        up? He'd taken the wheel while you slept off a
        night of boozing with Philby? Right?

GUY   Mm. Philbers, if anything, drinks even more
        than you do.

REES   Really?

GUY   A sorry sight.

REES   With typical gallantry you claim diplomatic
        immunity for yourself, friend and Lincoln
        Continental but the Governor of Virginia
        complains officially to the British Embassy so
        next boat home? Is that right?

GUY   Broadly speaking. High on a hill truth stands of
        course but yes, yes, mm.

REES   Next I get a wire saying you'll be arriving at
        Southampton Saturday. Can you come down
        today, Sunday, it's urgent.

GUY   And here I am.

REES   Mm. Loaded with presents—plastic washing-up
        bowls, toys for the children so captivating their
        old ones are quite forgotten—

GUY   My bounden duty as a godfather. Your wife by
        the bye thinks I got here too soon too. Vee put
        out she is.

REES   Nonsense. Margie's very fond of you, Guy.
        Really. You know she is.

GUY   No, at best I'd say your other half's trained
        herself to tolerate me. For Margie I'm one of

	those acquired tastes like Cod Liver Oil or Liquafruta.
REES	What's more you impress us by looking so clean.
GUY	Good Lord.
REES	And you're much slimmer too.
GUY	Mm. Lost a stone.
REES	But beyond all else there seems to be a sort of glow or shine inside you—like a child before Christmas or the summer holidays.
GUY	Well, that's coming home! I'm just so damn glad to be back in dear old Blighty. That's what it is. Believe me.

(Pause.) |
REES	So you did exaggerate? There's nothing urgent or special about your visit after all?
GUY	Averting World War Three isn't urgent, let alone special, oh, no, pudding, no!
REES	Don't be silly—even you can't imagine this can make any difference to that!
GUY	I try to be of relevance!
REES	You always have, yes. But I'm right, aren't I? Don't wriggle. This is a smokescreen isn't it?
GUY	No. *(Pause.)* No!
REES	Very well. In that case what are you going to do with it? It's been rejected—if your ambassador wouldn't even agree to read it let alone approve it—
GUY	Exactly, precisely ! So to hell with him! The whole shoot—all of 'em—timeserving flunkeys! I'm going to press this despatch right through and up to the Foreign Secretary's desk—oh, yes.
REES	But how? How on earth? Oh, Guy, don't be absurd—this is moonshine.

GUY   Chums, dear. It is possible, you know, to work
           through other than office channels. One has old
           acquaintances of some substance in various
           positions who shall not be forgot.

REES   Nor be allowed to forget, I daresay?

GUY   That's right. They'll help. (*Grin.*) You really are
           my *alter ego*, Rees. Know me only too well,
           don't you? Many owe me much from when I
           worked for the BBC—not least certain eager
           young deputies panting for a first airing on *The
           Week in Westminster.*

REES   (*laughing*) Whom you rogered so jollily? I am
           familiar with your career, Guy—

GUY   As I with yours—though we must admit, you
           haven't quite lived up to your early promise.
           Your Celtic eloquence coupled with your
           grammar-school charm deceived us all, I
           suspect.

REES   I doubt that. However—you hope to use this
           memo to revenge yourself on the entire foreign
           service—is that it?—for not taking you to its
           bosom and recognizing in you the intellectual
           giant and political Tiresias you really are?

           (*Pause.*)

GUY   Not at all. We need the truth known. Where it
           matters. Before it's too late. Do you want
           Britain to remain America's running dog?
           Because that's how we're seen in the Far East,
           believe me. And under a Labour government
           too. The shame of it, Rees, the shame of it.

REES   I've never been quite sure where to look when
           you become sincere, Guy.

           (*Pause.*)

GUY   Perhaps you are a lost cause, after all?

REES   Oh, come along! Enough flannel now! If
           something's got to be said, say it. Let's let the

breeze blow the smoke away, shall we? Let the
dog see the rabbit—righto?

GUY   And the rabbit the dog?

REES   Whichever way round you wish. Come on,
Guy. The real reason? The genuine gen?

            (*Pause.*)

GUY   This is of course strictly classified, indeed most
secret—

REES   My discretion's worn pretty well, wouldn't you
say? Over the years—lasted a long time—since
before the war—?

GUY   I should hope it had. As a fellow-worker.

REES   Uh ha.

GUY   No need to dampen your camiknicks, sweetie—
this isn't your call to action.

REES   I never thought it was!

GUY   Go on! Of course you did. But not to worry,
comrade. You may sleep on, carry on snorting
in the seven sleeper's den though seven is a very
modest estimate for the number of chaps I've in
fact recruited for the cause.

REES   Guy! Guy! Once and for all I never accepted
your invitation!

GUY   Sorry, dear heart, you're re-jigging history as
per usual.

REES   I'm not!

GUY   Pull the other tit, toothsome—no one refuses.
Can't be done. Isn't on. The invitation *is* the
engagement.

REES   I don't accept that! I never have!

GUY   Be that as it may that's how it is.

            (*Pause.*)

REES	You always say that, always! That's been your argument ever since—
GUY	Because it's bloody true! Good god, man! The KGB has never issued an invitation yet without first vetting the candidate. I had to put in a full report on you—background, education, prospects. You were accepted. You're on file as having said yes.
REES	Then the record's wrong!
GUY	I wouldn't say so. No, not in essence. No. No—you've always had the heart of the matter in you. And besides we're indissolubly linked, are we not? By time and hopes—and fears? After all, you could've spilt the beans ages ago—you still could, I suppose? But no, no— inconceivable—not—
REES	Guy—you're babbling.
GUY	Me? No, duckie, never. No, I'm asking myself could I imagine your hand, yours stretching out to the telephone to ring up the police—
REES	(*overlap*) Of course not! Oh, Guy! And why should I? Or would I? And don't quote Morgan Forster at me—we all know it by heart!
GUY	But one cannot quote him too often.
REES	You can!
GUY	Yes! He's the nub—the still point. 'If I had to choose between betraying my country and—'
REES	No! Come on Guy! Since you say it isn't me its got to be you. You've been called to action in some way? Is that what you're working round to?
GUY	Never been out of action. Busied myself for the cause these seventeen years off and on.
REES	Yes!
	(*Pause.*)

GUY	While in Washington I stayed with dear old Kim.
REES	Mm—I thought that peculiar.
GUY	Double bluff. You don't care for Kim, do you?
REES	I hardly know him.
GUY	He knows all about you—sends his regards.
REES	Does he?
GUY	What an intelligencer—yes, I couldn't find any digs so Kim kindly said muck in. Normally of course senior oppos tend not to doss down together—
REES	Philby wanted to keep an eye on you? Stop you swanning off downtown?
GUY	Oh, I never thought of that. That may have been in Kim's sagacious mind, yes. Anyway we decided what with our past links—Cambridge, Spain, SOE—all common knowledge doubtless fully on file—after all, it was I who got young Philbers into MI6 in the first place—on mature consideration we thought what the hell, Archie, what the hell? Indeed on balance we thought it looked better rather than worse.
REES	So blatant as to be innocent?
GUY	Precisely. Ever my style, wouldn't you say?
REES	Yes. Yes.

(*Pause.*)

GUY	Kim then took me into his confidence re. 'Homer'.
REES	Homer who?
GUY	Oh, no, not a Yank. Codename Homer. The cryptonym for our mutual friend—Donald.

(*Pause.* REES *has frozen.* GUY *notices.*)

REES	That bastard!

GUY	Donald? Do you think so? Sometimes. It depends. He can give one the pip—but who doesn't?—I buggered him once you know and all the thanks I got was—I quote—'I'm not sure sodomy's my cup of tea after all.' Jolly ungrateful to one who has since serviced ninety nine per cent of the Senior Service to their entire satisfaction. Yes, Kim told me about Homer because he felt, along with his mentors, that I could be of material help.
REES	What's Maclean done? (REES *swallows his whisky, reaches for the bottle again.*)
GUY	Well, he's fully recovered from the bends. Why *do* we all drink so much? (*Grin.*) Don't tell me it's the strain of the bifurcated lives we lead? No, Donald hasn't done anything of note recently—someone else has. A whisper floats in the air. He's come under suspicion. I've been detailed to bail him out.
REES	How?
GUY	Hold his hand, take him on hols. We can't have the dear fellow put through the mangle by MI5—gee whiz—stuffed to the gunwales though it be with old shipmates.
REES	It wasn't me. Maclean may try to tell you it was but it wasn't. That I swear to you, Guy. Have you seen him yet? Has he—?
GUY	No. We're lunching tomorrow. You? I didn't dream of it. Never crossed my mind. You?
REES	No. It's a bee he's got. Quite untrue. Baseless. He came up to me at the Gargoyle Club—
GUY	Ah, that's what Margie meant, was it? About—?
REES	Yes! Yes. He was hopelessly drunk—
GUY	When was this?
REES	Last November. Just after you'd gone to America.

GUY   He's dried out since. And had his head shrunk,
           too. One hears he's quite pretty again really.

REES   He wasn't then. He was pie-eyed, livid yellow—
           he came up to our table, pointed at me and
           shouted: 'You used to be one of us but you
           ratted.' I got up to hit him. He saved me the
           trouble by passing out.

GUY   Good Lord.

REES   But the question is what did he mean by it? I
           admit I've always assumed he joined the cause
           when you did—

GUY   No. Later. He now heads the American section
           in London—he's risen far. Lived up to his early
           promise. Fancy you splitting on him? Naughty.

REES   Don't tease. I said! I didn't—

GUY   Hence my concern, sausage.

REES   Oh for heaven's sake!

GUY   Relaxez-vous. We know who dunnit. It wasn't
           over here. No, sir, no, siree.

REES   Well, that's something.

           (*Enter* MARGIE.)

GUY   Quite, if we blame anyone it's the new head of
           the CIA—

REES   Oh, hello, Margie.

GUY   (*to her at once*) My dear, Rees was only this
           minute explaining about what you said—about
           that man in the Gargoyle. Extraordinary. Just
           shows what booze can do to a fellow. Am I to
           infer it's time for me to tell the girls their
           bedtime story?

MARGIE   Please. They keep asking.

GUY   Righty-ho-ho-ho.

REES   Nothing too stimulating, Guy.

GUY   Fear not, paterfamilias. I may simply sing to
           them.

MARGIE   Oh, no!

GUY   How about 'I tort I taw a puddy-tat?' Or—hey,
           my Frankie Laine's rather good. Jezebel. (*Sings.*)
           'If ever the devil was born without a pair of
           horns, it was you, Jezebel, it was you. Like a
           demon love possessed me, you obsessed me
           constantly—'

           (*Exit* GUY *singing.* MARGIE *picks up the scattered
           toys.*)

MARGIE   He's worse than ever.

REES   His fingernails are cleaner.

MARGIE   So he did ask you about that man—?

REES   Rather. But that isn't anything to do with why
           he's come down.

MARGIE   Oh, good.

REES   It's as we thought—Guy as family friend,
           responsible godfather etcetera. Oh, and he did
           want my opinion of his memo, of course.

MARGIE   What's it like? It seems rather long.

REES   Let's say it's typically Guy.

MARGIE   Oh, dear.

REES   I can't see it saving him from the sack at the
           Foreign Office, Margie. Come here, girl. You
           mustn't mind about Guy.

MARGIE   Oh, Rees.

           (*Kiss.*)

REES   Okay?

MARGIE   Mm. Mm.

REES   Oh, there is one thing—he says the girls
           shouldn't have called the cat Burgess. Infradig. I

told him he ought to be flattered—it's a very handsome pussy.

(*They laugh.*)

MARGIE   They wanted to go to bed in their blue jeans. Oh, you know that washing-up bowl he's brought—he says it's made of a plastic you can drive a car over.

REES   Go on!

MARGIE   Mm. You can squash it flat but it's so springy it'll still flip back into shape.

REES   Dieu!

MARGIE   Or so he says. I thought I'd take him at his word.

REES   Drive the Ford over it?

MARGIE   Rather fun. Tomorrow morning. Before he goes. The children'll love it. I'm so glad—

(*Re-enter* GUY.)

GUY   Jumped the gun! Fast asleep. No need for song or fable. Snoring their heads off. Little beasts looked like angels.

REES   Been quite a day for them.

GUY   Me too. All that tadpoling. Golly gum drops.

MARGIE   Supper won't be long. I promise. But well, you know us—(*Exit* MARGIE *with toys.*)

GUY   Well, well, well, pick up sticks. (*He pours himself Chablis.*)

REES   You were blaming the CIA?

GUY   Mm—the new head thereof. Mm. On taking over he started—reasonably enough—to open cupboards. Whoopsadaisy—what have we here? Several well-preserved skeletons. One of which was that while in Washington at the end of the war a British envoy answering to Donald's codename—i.e. Homer—had procured a higher grade of official pass to the US Atomic Commission than he was in fact entitled to.

REES   Oh. Tricky.

GUY   Mm. Mind you, it was in its time—
                '44 – '48—Donald's most fruitful acquisition. If there is now atomic equilibrium between East and West—and there is—one could say it is largely due to Donald's sterling efforts. Thanks to him our world is that much safer from US imperialism.

REES   You hope.

GUY   Don't you?

REES   Of course.

GUY   Anyway, come Good Friday last—Yankee-doodle panic stations! The CIA officially informs MI6—thank heavens we'd got Kim in situ—'Look, fella, we guess you dropped a bad apple in our basket some time back and maybe he's still in yours—have a look-see, will ya?'

REES   Your American accent's disgusting.

GUY   So are Americans. Well, of course, at this, poor old Kim has no choice but to sound the alarm or look rather iffy himself. Upshot? FO internal security has now got a short list of six gorgeous beasts whose curricula vitae click alongside Donald's.

REES   Philby's muddied the waters?

GUY   To give us time.

REES   But Maclean's on that short list—supplied by Philby?

GUY   Oh, yes. Kim couldn't in all conscience leave him off it, could he?

REES   I suppose not—no.

GUY	Hence me here.
REES	You're saying you've come home deliberately?
GUY	But of course.
REES	And that speeding offence?
GUY	Oh, that was a pleasure to commit. You know how funereal their driving is. I hit the ton three times running with this prettiest of pump boys snuggled up beside me—the traffic cops had a fit—the Governor of Virginia his first-ever orgasm—he had to look up what it was in the Kinsey Report. Bliss! Kim was awfully proud of me.
REES	He ordered you to do it?
GUY	Oh, yes. He's senior to me now. Disgrace yourself dear boy, were his words. You see, security-wise, I'm Stainless Steven. Whiter than white!
REES	Really?
GUY	So Kim says—he should know. That's why they've decided I'm the ideal person to help Donald.
REES	They?
GUY	Kim and his fellow-officers in the States. Mind you, *entre-nous,* I suspected another hand as well—and I was right. Which is really, really why I've come down here.
REES	Really?
GUY	Mm. Yes, it is.
REES	Well?
	(*Pause.*)
GUY	I saw Anthony last night.
REES	I thought we weren't to mention him?
GUY	I can. As I thought, it was he who first suggested I should be the one to help Donald.

REES	He put your name up to his controller and—?
GUY	We don't use that word.
REES	Too accurate?
GUY	No—enemy jargon. As you know perfectly well. We're a service like any other, with ranks. No opprobium at any level even if like you, you remain an ageing subaltern-in-waiting.
REES	Not again!
GUY	You can't have your cake and eat it, Rees. You're either with us or else. I wouldn't be telling you all this, would I, if I thought otherwise? (*Pause.*) Would I?
	(*Pause.*)
REES	You might if you'd got to, whether you liked it or not.
GUY	Why should that be?
REES	Because I know so much already?
GUY	That isn't a threat, I trust?
REES	Oh, Guy, Guy. Why can't we simply, finally agree we're both enlightened, both self-interested? And on that realistic basis of mutual—
GUY	But we aren't! I'm enlightened—you're self-interested!
REES	No!
GUY	Oh, yes! If you aren't for, you're against! When's the next train back to town?
REES	(*glance at watch*) You've just missed it.
GUY	Green Line bus?
REES	Gone too. Come on, sit down, you don't mean it.
GUY	I do! I damn well do! I've always hoped—hope against hope—that one day you'll commit

yourself! Completely, without reserve, proviso, equivocation! But do you? No! Fat lot you care! Okay—I give up. You *are* a lost cause—the revolution's better off without you. Mr Nobody changes trains again—you bloody, bloody fellow-traveller—ugh! And I've told you too much, indulged you, trusted you over and over out of hope—hope you'd be true one day, one day to your real self! But oh no! What a fool I've been—what a misguided, naïve—

REES   Oh, for heaven's sake—sit down! You *can* trust me. You know you can. You've got to anyway—no choice. But beyond that—as a friend you can. As a friend, Guy.

GUY   That isn't enough.

REES   My God, how can you of all people—?

GUY   Not now I've put myself and my real friends in pawn—to you!—hocked us all out of—

REES   Oh, don't, don't say that or you'll tempt me! (*Pause—control.*) Just sit down and have a proper drink. That wine's too acid for you. (*He pours* GUY *a generous whisky and pushes it across to him.* GUY *does not take it.*) Let's be quite clear—I used to think as you do—I still sympathize with your ideals though I hate what happens to them when they're realized—but you can trust me, you can continue to speak freely to me, your secrets are safe with me and simply as your friend I'm insulted if you think they aren't—all right? (*Pause.* GUY *nods.*) Thank you. And don't sulk. Next I shall mention Anthony. He is of some importance, isn't he? To us both. Not least because you named him as part of your sales patter when you tried to recruit me.

GUY   Ducky—I only mentioned Anthony after you said yes to joining us.

REES   No!

GUY	Yes! Your memory. Somewhat selective. (*He takes the whisky, downs it in one gulp. Pause.*)
REES	Anyway Anthony's now persuaded you back home?
GUY	Yes. As nanny to Donald.
REES	I'd have thought Maclean could've looked after himself.
GUY	Not with a dodgy, vengeful, very pregnant wife, he can't.
REES	Oh, I see. Yes. She might not wish him to go anywhere—for any length of time. Might she?
GUY	So we assume. Melinda's a poppet but—and with Donald himself only just released from the funny farm—
REES	Yes. I can see you having to be a rather firm sort of nanny. (*Pause.*) Don't you? (*Pause.*) Have another. (*He pushes the bottle of Bells' to* GUY, *who does not respond.*) We sank a bottle of this that evening.
GUY	We didn't.
REES	I'm sure we did—
GUY	No—
REES	I remember distinctly! Good Lord, I'm hardly likely to forget, am I? It was quite—after all it isn't every day your greatest friend tells you he's a secret agent and wants you to join him. You do tend to remember such things—
GUY	Johnny Jameson. Usquebagh. It was.
REES	All right! We drank Irish whiskey. Who cares?
GUY	God's in the detail—Kim always says.
REES	Does he? Fine. Bully for him.
GUY	Know your onions, cultivate total recall, look out for the meaningless incident—those are his watchwords.

REES	I daresay maxims if that kind are pertinent for him.
GUY	They are. Yes.
REES	And for such as he.
GUY	Yes. Mm. True. (*Pause.*)
REES	Well, my memory may occasionally play me false but one thing's plain—Anthony still loves you or he wouldn't have—
GUY	I said don't speak of him!
REES	And I said I was going to, didn't I? Didn't I?
GUY	Oh, very well.
REES	After all love's a social quality if it's anything? Human cement, wouldn't you say? For Anthony to arrange your recall strikes me as the action of a lover. So fond he must see you whatever the cost.
GUY	Balls. It was done out of purely professional considerations—nothing else. (*He seizes the bottle and pours himself a glass.*)
REES	Such things get interwoven, don't you find?
GUY	Not with us.
REES	I don't believe you. I've seen how Anthony's cared for you over the years. That's no secret, is it? How he's condoned your chronic infidelities—
GUY	Who's talking?
REES	Me—about you—now—
GUY	The randiest Welshman since Lloyd George! Good God, man—(*laughing*)—legend has it Oxford bluestockings turned to blancmange at your approach! And when you hit town as assistant editor of the *Spectator* no less—boy oh

boy gosh—leading lady novelists fell over
themselves to—(*self-interruption*)—have you ever
told Margie what a universal steam plough you
used to be?

REES   Yes. Guy?

GUY   Something?

REES   I was speaking about you and Anthony. (*Pause.*
            GUY *shrugs.*) He told me once he didn't mind
            what you did with other people—you were
            always true in your fashion, he said—but his
            face was a mask.

GUY   His po-face? As of a skull with toothache?

REES   Mm. Nursing the hurt.

GUY   (*huge laugh*) Tosh! Sentimental lending library
            tosh! Shopgirl romancing rubbish, Rees!
            Anthony and I agreed years ago to have it both
            ways. She's as louche as me, ducky—oh I know
            her public style's Lady Bracknell with knobs on
            but when the lights are low and the company's
            lower—then 'many a fickle makes a fuckle'
            Antonia says. She it was coined the phrase.

REES   But even so he still loves you?

GUY   Of course.

REES   And you? Do you—?

GUY   He's my oldest friend. As ever.

REES   Thanks. That's all I needed to know. As escort
            to Maclean what—?

GUY   I simply see him on his way—nothing else.

REES   Where to? You haven't said, have you? Beyond
            the iron curtain?

GUY   I'd have thought that went without saying. Mm.
            And heaven his destination. Yes.

            (*Pause.*)

REES   I imagine they're proud of him in Moscow?

GUY	Proud of us all.
REES	His arrival ought to be quite a propaganda coup, wouldn't you say?
GUY	Oh, no—they don't think like that. No. It's just what they'd do for any comrade. Welcome home.
	(*Pause.*)
REES	Is there a plan of escape?
GUY	More or less.
REES	Who's in charge of it—you?
GUY	Me? I just obey orders.
REES	Then it must be Anthony?
GUY	You've said it.
	(*Pause.*)
REES	Is Maclean being watched?
GUY	Oh, yes, all six on the short list are.
REES	But no formal questioning so far?
GUY	Good Lord, no. But it'll come. We don't know when.
REES	Isn't it important to find out?
GUY	Anthony again—thanks to his long-standing association with Five. And Six, come to that.
REES	He's the key to the whole operation?
GUY	Always has been.
	(*Pause.*)
REES	How far do you think you'll have to go with Maclean?
	(*Pause.*)
GUY	As far as—necessary.
REES	(*assent noise*) Uh—hm. Is there in fact enough evidence to put him on trail?

GUY	Anthony doubts it. I agree. There's no prima-facie case against Donald. Not in English law. But that doesn't mean MI5 can't grill him, does it?
REES	No. If there were a case in law he could be hanged, of course?

(*Pause.*)

GUY	We all could. Or serve thirty years at His Majesty's pleasure. Speaking for myself I'd prefer to be topped. What about you?

(*Pause.*)

REES	Shall we go in?

(*Pause.*)

GUY	You're right, Rees, quite right. I did have to tell you all this—no choice. Didn't want to, but the fact is, we're entirely in your hands—all of us, me, Donald, Kim, Anthony. Promise me, honour bright, you'll keep—radio silence shall we say—whatever happens?
REES	I have. I will—provided—fair do's—you keep me fully briefed. You aren't thinking of going too, I hope?
GUY	Heavens no! It'd break Anthony's heart.
REES	I'm sure.
GUY	You know everything about us. It's Anthony I'm thinking of basically. Kim can look after himself—after all he's right at the centre of things.
REES	And Donald will have gone?
GUY	Quite. But Anthony's—well—more vulnerable—security-wise. Oh, he's still on excellent terms with lots of people in the Service but it stands to reason he can't know everything as it occurs—not like Kim. So there's bound to be some risk for dear old Ant when the news gets out.

REES	And for you? I'd have thought?
GUY	I shall have resigned from the FO by then.
REES	That won't help.
GUY	My next job will. With the *Telegraph*.
REES	Go on, You said it was just a long shot—a faint possibility—
GUY	No! Wrong end! You've got the—yes, it's certain-sure! They've asked me, not t'other way round, love.
REES	Oh!
GUY	Fleeters Streeters—here I come! Okay? Point taken?
REES	If that's how it is, of course—yes. And I do see that as their new diplomatic correspondent you'd be well placed to conduct a most misleading investigation into the mystery of the missing diplomat you yourself helped escape. Yes. I can see that. Mm.
GUY	Yes. Rather a challenge, what? Not to say a hoot. (*Laughs.*) Superb cover, too. (*New tone.*) And if they should come to you as well, Rees?
REES	I'll cope.
GUY	How?
	(*Pause.*)
REES	Oh, I'm sure I can cobble something together. It has been said I have imagination. Something along the lines of—oh, I don't know—how you came down here to beg complicity from me while pretending you were genuinely concerned about the imminent likelihood of a third world war—
GUY	I am! You can't—
REES	And how—as ever—you were not averse to a spot of emotional blackmail—to put it politely—

about old times stiffened with a snort of
intellectual dishonesty such as only Cambridge
can supply—

GUY   You're teasing me, aren't you?

REES   I hope so. Think so. But how eventually, like a
Soho showgirl, you gave nothing away while
apparently revealing all.

GUY   I've told you everything, love! Everything!
You're completely informed—in the know—up
to date. And will be kept so. Okey-dokey?

(*Pause.*)

REES   Then of course. Of course! I shan't say
anything—to anyone—I promise. Of course.

GUY   Good. In the end all we've got are our friends.

REES   When I said that, it wasn't enough, you said.

GUY   I didn't mean it.

REES   It certainly didn't sound like you.

GUY   Well. There we are. All's well—come full circle.
I can't tell you how much it means to me to
know—come what may—that Anthony's secret
is safe. With you. You're a friend indeed. (*He
kisses* REES's *cheek, shakes his hand, pats his
shoulder.*) With guts as well as heart. Thank
you—so good—such a relief to have your word.
Your given word.

REES   You mean our old comrade Solomon Binding?

(*Both laugh.* GUY *raises his glass in a toast.*)

GUY   To Solly, Gawd bless him.

REES   (*replying*) To you. And Anthony.

GUY   (*return toast*) And to you, Rees.

(*Silence. Then they drink. From within the house the
dinner gong sounds. Lights fade.*)

END OF ACT ONE

ACT TWO

Scene One

Sunday night, 27th May—three weeks later.

Moonlight on the garden chairs and table together with a child's discarded cowboy hat and gun belt with toy revolver and holster. Whisky, soda siphon and tumbler on a tray. MARGIE *appears in her nightdress and dressing-gown carrying a candle in a glass bowl with* Picture Post *tucked under her arm. She sets down the bowl, produces matches and lights the candle. The phone rings off.* MARGIE *stiffens then goes quickly but after two rings it stops. So does* MARGIE. *She returns, clearly under strain. She sits and opens* Picture Post *determinedly. After a moment a car is heard off. The car stops but with the engine still running.*

REES	(*off*) Thank you. Good night. (*The car goes—*REES *calls.*) Margie?
MARGIE	I'm out here.
REES	(*off*) Oh, right you are.
	(*Pause.* REES *appears with a bulky briefcase and his suit jacket over his arm.*)
MARGIE	(*neutral*) It was such a lovely night.
REES	It was stifling in Oxford.
	(*They kiss briefly.*)
	Miss me?
MARGIE	Mm.
REES	Good girl. How are the children?
MARGIE	Asleep. Have you eaten?
REES	Sumptuously. All I need now is a snitch of that. (*He indicates the whisky and helps himself.*) How about you? Nightcap?
MARGIE	A small one.
	(*He pours it.*)
REES	I got beaten to the only taxi in Twyford. By two old biddies who ran like stags. Had to wait for it to come round again.
MARGIE	(*routine*) You really should learn to drive. With soda.

REES	So—well then, how's it been here—back at the ranch?
MARGIE	The girls have gone back to their old toys.
REES	(*laugh*) So much for poor old Guy and his munificence—
MARGIE	No.
REES	Mm?
MARGIE	(*blurt*) You must have got my messages? You must have!
REES	No. What?
MARGIE	I telephoned five times!
REES	To the Porter's Lodge?
MARGIE	Yes! The first time I left a message, the next I didn't, I did the next—I didn't the fourth time because I was too upset but the fifth I did—I said: 'When you do see Mr Rees, please, please tell him to ring home. It's quite important.'
REES	When was this?
MARGIE	Friday, Saturday, today! You're quite sure you did actually *go* to Oxford?
REES	(*laughing*) Oh, Margie love, of course. For heaven's sake, I delivered the annual report, didn't I? To the AGM. On Friday.
MARGIE	I thought you might've got involved—with Guy. Afterwards.
REES	(*puzzled*) Guy? I don't see—
MARGIE	You know how he monopolizes you. I supposed you must've gone on a bender. And that was why you never rang me back again.
REES	No—no—oh, my dear—no.
MARGIE	The porters kept saying they hadn't seen you.
REES	I was there—I promise.
MARGIE	Guy told me he might go down to Oxford. That was my first message. To warn you.

REES	Well, he didn't turn up.
MARGIE	Oh.
REES	Cross my heart. Honest Injun. Hope to die.
MARGIE	Oh.
REES	When did he say this? Threaten to descend on me?
MARGIE	Oh Friday—Friday morning. I'd just come in from shopping.
REES	(*pause*) The porters are usually reliable—they did have a temporary chap on.
MARGIE	Perhaps that explains it?
REES	It could. He wouldn't have known me necessarily. When did you phone—for the first time, I mean?
MARGIE	The minute Guy rang off. He'd wanted to speak to you of course. He pretended I did just as well but that was only politeness. It was about eleven—well, shortly after.
REES	And that's when you rang me?
MARGIE	Not quite. He went on and on. I suppose it must've been nearly quarter to twelve when I left my first message for you. Then Jimmy rang.
REES	Jimmy?
MARGIE	That sort of friend-cum-servant Guy's got.
REES	Oh, yes, of course. The peroxide bombshell.
MARGIE	I don't know what his hair's like.
REES	Mouse.
MARGIE	Mm?
REES	His hair—originally. Did he ring just after Guy?
MARGIE	Oh, no. On Saturday. That's when I rang you again.

REES	Ah.
MARGIE	Jimmy was in a terrific flap. He thought Guy might be here.
REES	He did? Why should he think that?
MARGIE	Because Guy hadn't come home, he said, all Friday night—
REES	Jimmy must be used to that sort of—
MARGIE	He said Guy always says if he'll be back or not.
REES	I'd take that with a pinch of salt—
MARGIE	He sounded—you know—hysterical—kept calling me darling though he doesn't know me, does he?
REES	He is rather ex-chorus boy. Guy probably spent a night on the tiles and has come home since.
MARGIE	He hasn't.
REES	Then he's made a weekend of it.
MARGIE	Jimmy rang again. This morning.
REES	(*carefully*) To say what?
MARGIE	He apologized and asked me please to forget he had ever telephoned. Ever. He sounded quite cool. Collected.
REES	Oh? (*Pause. As casually as he can:*) How did Guy himself sound when you talked to him?
MARGIE	He did most of the talking. With that thick voice. Rambling on—round and round.
REES	Drunk?
MARGIE	Like he was before he went to America.
REES	Oh, dear. We rather hoped he stopped all that, didn't we?
MARGIE	You got him back on spirits.
REES	True. I expect he was drunk. Oh dear, oh dear. *Mea culpa.*
	(*Pause.*)

MARGIE	He said you'd know what he was talking about. It certainly didn't make sense to me.
REES	Oh?
MARGIE	He kept saying he was going to surprise everybody. 'Tell Rees I'm about to astonish the world. Rees'll understand. No one better.' Even though you and he had parted company politically-speaking he said—and even though you'd ratted on them—
REES	(*sharp anger*) He said that?
MARGIE	Twice. So I said please, if it's about that man in that club it's nothing to do with me, I don't want anything to do with it—he would have to speak to you about that.
REES	You should've put the phone down on him!
MARGIE	I wanted to.
REES	You were brought up far too respectably, my love.
MARGIE	I think I must've been. That's when he said he might go and see you.
REES	And that was all?
MARGIE	More or less—in the meantime 'cheerio for a while' and oodles of hugs and kisses to the children—you know how he talks. Oh—and you wouldn't forget your mutual friend—old Solomon Binding, would you? He said that three times. Who's Solomon Binding?
REES	Oh, darling, darling, don't you know?
MARGIE	No.
REES	Really? It's such a hoary old joke—it means giving your word—your solemn and binding word.
MARGIE	You've promised Guy something?
REES	Hey—you're too quick.

MARGIE   What? What have you promised him? What?

REES   Steady on, girl—no need to get worked up—

MARGIE   (*overlap*) You would be! Because since then the
         phone's gone four times more! Once at two in
         the morning! But whoever it is always rings off
         when I pick up the receiver. It went again just
         now but stopped after two dring-drings. What's
         happening, Rees? Is it to do with Guy? It must
         be—surely? He said you'd understand and
         'you'd promised. What? What is it? Is it some
         nasty pansy thing?

REES   Shush—

MARGIE   I hoped he'd stay in America for ever! I can't
         tell you how my heart sank when he—

REES   You've no reason to be jealous or afraid of Guy,
         darling. None. Guy is simply my friend in the
         best, best sense of the word.

MARGIE   He's always taking your arm, patting your
         shoulder—

REES   Just camaraderie. It doesn't mean anything.
         You didn't mind his being Thomas's godfather,
         did you?

MARGIE   I swallowed my pride. Told myself what you've
         just told me: they're such friends.

REES   Oh, my love. You should've said.

MARGIE   I didn't dare. You and Guy—you're older.

REES   My dear little girl—(*He sighs. Pause.*) I think I
         know what he was talking about—yes, that'll
         have been it, yes! Silly of me not to realize
         straightaway—yes! How daft—of course!

MARGIE   What?

REES   He must've decided to take that job with the
         Telegraph. That'll be it.

MARGIE   Oh, no, Rees! No! It sounded much more
         important than that!

REES   Nonesense, ducky. For Guy having to take a job
              with the *Daily Telegraph* of all papers would be
              cataclysmic. Some of his more puritanical
              friends would think he'd gone over to the
              enemy! And when he said I'd understand what
              he meant was he'd remembered I'd told him the
              rather obvious truth that a journalist doesn't
              necessarily have to hold the same views as the
              paper he works for. That's what he meant—of
              course. Aren't we dumb clucks? Good Lord—

              (*He laughs.* MARGIE *doesn't.*)

MARGIE   But no one says 'goodbye' just because they're
              going to work for the *Daily Telegraph*!

REES   Guy would! That's exactly how he'd put it. It
              would be a big crisis for him, believe me, to
              have to work out of necessity for a right-wing
              paper.

MARGIE   (*sharper*) And when he said you'd ratted like that
              other man said?

REES   Margie, Margie—all he meant there was I'm no
              longer as committed to pure Marxist socialism
              as he is. Which is perfectly true. So he throws a
              few bad eggs. All we socialists do. Just as we
              love ye olde argy-bargy hustings rhetoric—lovely
              radical hot air—

MARGIE   Oh, please—I want, please, I want to believe
              you, please.

REES   Well, you can—you must.

MARGIE   But I don't. Don't, don't, don't, Rees.

REES   Why not—why not?

MARGIE   Because I had Guy on the phone! It wasn't just
              about a stupid job! Whatever it was it was more
              than that! And those other phone calls. To me it
              feels, well, almost—criminal. And you won't tell
              me and you must! Mustn't you? If you won't all
              I can suppose is—is—is your friendship for
              Guy's more important than anything else—

REES	My dear—
	(*The phone rings, off. Both freeze.*)
MARGIE	(*whisper*) Shall I go?
REES	No. I will. And if I find it's some practical joker who's worried you stiff, I'll damn well give him—
	(*The phone stops, off. Pause.*)
MARGIE	Just like before.
REES	No wonder you're on edge. (*Embrace.*) Oh, my darling.
MARGIE	Tell me.
	(*Pause.*)
REES	Indoors. In bed.
MARGIE	No. Here. Now.
REES	It's now or never?
MARGIE	No. Now.
	(*Pause.*)
REES	Well, of course, we first met a long time ago— Guy and I—he used to drive over from Cambridge to Oxford, he was a friend of Maurice Bowra's—
MARGIE	I know that!
REES	You asked, Margie!
MARGIE	Not to be told things I already know!
REES	Very well, but they're still part of the picture. We met again—later—in London. When I had a flat in Ebury Street—
MARGIE	And Guy lived just round the corner—yes!
REES	Right you are, you know everything, heard it all before. I'll stop!
MARGIE	No! Just tell me what matters, not the geography!

REES   But it does matter! The geography. History
            often is geography. If I hadn't run into Guy
            again—oh God! Look, Margie my sweet, I want
            to tell you but how can you possibly
            understand? How?

MARGIE   By having to. Are you trying to tell me you
            did—did go to bed with Guy or something—
            after all? Oh—

REES   (laughing, relieved) Good Lord no! Oh, my love, if
            it were as easy as that—

MARGIE   Easy! He wrote that beastly letter telling you not
            to marry me!

REES   Telling me not to marry anyone! That's why I
            showed it to you. He didn't mean you
            personally, Margie, he was talking about me,
            the wisdom of my marrying in general. Me, not
            you. He said I had no conventional sense of
            identity—perfectly true, I'd told him!—that I'd
            got the morals of a Cardiff alley cat enlightened
            by David Hume—how I was not so much Mr
            Norris as Mr Nobody—

MARGIE   No. You've forgotten—it wasn't all about you.
            There was plenty about me though he'd never
            met me. About how young I was, how
            infatuated I must be, how I couldn't possibly be
            your intellectual equal—I was bourgeois,
            provincial—a banker's daughter from the Wirral
            of all places—imagine. Just a wartime thing.

            (Pause.)

REES   I shouldn't've shown it to you—how could I
            expect you to understand? At nineteen? But I
            swear to you I never had any kind of affair with
            Guy, darling. Once you make it clear that sort
            of thing isn't your cup of tea Guy accepts it.
            Sexually he can be perfectly civilized, believe
            me.

MARGIE   You know so much about him.

REES   I wouldn't say that.

MARGIE	Well, since it wasn't anything—like that between you—you can tell me what it really is, can't you?
REES	I was trying. Mind you, people like Guy do love to make conquests of every kind—not simply physical ones—spiritual ones, philosophical ones, intellectual ones, political ones and in those days we did see eye to eye politically.
MARGIE	Oh, yes—anybody who was anybody was a socialist then, yes, I know.
REES	It wasn't just a fashion, love.
MARGIE	No. You all meant it.
REES	We were right to be horrified. It's too easy to jeer now. The thirties were filthy, filthy times. You didn't need even half a brain or half a heart to know that! Nor did it matter what class or school—
MARGIE	Yes, I know all that, yes! When you said—?
REES	What?
MARGIE	When you said Guy conquered you—?
REES	I didn't!
MARGIE	You did!
REES	No! I said people like Guy love to make conquests.
MARGIE	Same thing.
REES	No! Not at all.
MARGIE	I do know how you put things, Rees. And why tell me about the thirties? I know about them. I was alive then. We did have the thirties up in Liverpool. And I am capable of understanding—
REES	Of course you are. I wasn't saying—
MARGIE	Well then! (*Freeze.*) Shush—is that—? No. I thought it was the phone again.
REES	Do you want me to go on?

Margie	Mm. But don't lecture me.
Rees	I was only—you see this time you've really got to appreciate the background, my dear.
Margie	Well I do.
Rees	I hope so—you see as idealists we were all such worldly-wise virgins—so fervent—it's difficult to credit now—now we're all starting to get fed up with socialist austerity and state welfare. We were so committed, egalitarian, so anti-fascist, so internationalist, communist—the Soviet Union, for instance, we all saw literally as our promised land where the corn was immortal wheat grown to a correct five year plan inevitably and the dust and stones of Moscow—our holy city—were precious as gold—people usually went to Russia in the Long Vac, it was virtually obligatory, some actually kissed the ground when they got there—smile—and what we called the masses, or the workers, or the proletariat—how old-fashioned such terms sound now—seemed to us then, especially if they were Russian, to be angels and seraphim as it were and their children—the fruit of free love—they were moving jewels. Can you understand that? How it was?
Margie	Like watching an old film.
Rees	Which looks silly now but wasn't then. So it seemed perfectly reasonable even if I was surprised when Guy chose to confide in me. And it was said in absolute confidence—long before I'd met you—and that's why I've never told a soul. Not even you.
Margie	But I matter more now—do I?
Rees	You always have.
Margie	Well?
Rees	I'm not sure you'll like knowing.
Margie	Let's see, shall we?

REES	(*drinks, then*) Very well. One evening in Ebury Street—this was in 1936—I'd just broken off with someone who'd been awfully fond of me and I of her come to that—Guy told me he'd joined the Comintern.
MARGIE	What's that?
REES	(*laugh*) Oh, no! No. I tell you at last and you don't understand!
MARGIE	You could explain.
REES	Yes. Well—oh dear—(*stops laughing*)—yes, Comintern is shorthand for the Communist International—if it were Christian it would be a missionary movement. It spreads the Marxist gospel beyond the Soviet Union, liaises with all other Communist Parties, funds popular fronts and has also been known variously as the NKVD, OGPU or KGB—
MARGIE	Is it good or bad?
REES	Well that rather depends—it also recruits intelligence workers.
MARGIE	Spies?
REES	We only call them that when we don't sympathize with their ideals. Assuming they aren't doing it for money, of course.
MARGIE	Guy's a spy?
REES	(*assenting nod*) You could say that—mm.
	(*Pause.*)
MARGIE	Why did he tell you?
REES	Frankly at first I thought it was a joke—one of his fabrications—
MARGIE	Please answer! Why did he—?
REES	I am trying to tell you! But it's got to be seen in context! And in perspective, too!
MARGIE	(*complete override*) Why did he tell you?

REES   To get if off his chest!

MARGIE   Oh, Rees.

REES   What? What more do you want? (MARGIE *does
            not reply. Pause.*) Don't cry. We were drinking.
            Irish whiskey—as it happened. We got through
            the bottle. The sun went down. I brought his
            confession on myself really, I suppose. I
            challenged him to explain to me why just about
            then he'd become so inexplicably patriotic,
            blimpish, jingoistic—he'd decorated his bedroom
            in red, white and blue, even had a huge White
            Ensign as a bedspread— a friend had pinched it
            from the *Ark Royal*, he said. He was pro-Nazi,
            pro the Raj in India and was working with the
            Anglo-German Fellowship—Guy of all people! I
            couldn't understand such a reversal so I said
            'Guy, please tell me why you've rejected
            communism because your new fascist
            enthusiasms frankly nauseate me. Why?' And
            that's when he told me. Told me he wasn't
            really a turncoat at all, quite the reverse. He
            was working under cover for the Comintern.
            They'd ordered him to pretend to change his
            tune, as you might say.

MARGIE   (*tears on her cheeks*) Why?

REES   I don't understand your question any more.

MARGIE   You do. You must. It's still the same one. Why
            did he tell you?

REES   Because I asked!

MARGIE   But Guy never gives anything away for nothing.

REES   He does! He's the most generous of men!

MARGIE   No—there's always a price. Haven't you
            noticed? Oh, he sings for his supper but you
            jolly well provide the supper.

REES   Well, that's fair enough, surely?

MARGIE   Perhaps. But it means I've only heard the half
            of it so far, doesn't it? He had no need to tell

you he was a spy just because you wondered about his new political views.

REES   Well he must've found it necessary—we'd nearly finished the bottle. So've I. Look. Anyway the fact of it is he told me out of friendship, Margie. Pure friendship, honest friendship, sheer unadulterated—he didn't want anything in— return.

(*The phone rings, off.*)

(*Rising too quickly.*) I'll go. (*He sways.*)

MARGIE   No. I will.

REES   No—

(*Exit* MARGIE. *This time the phone continues to ring long enough to be answered.* REES *sits again. Tears in his eyes.*)

You've gone too, haven't you? 'Cheerio' for a while indeed. Oh, Guy—

(*Pause. Re-enter* MARGIE.)

MARGIE   It's for you.

REES   Who?

MARGIE   He wouldn't tell me. Like you.

REES   Not Guy? Nor Jimmy?

MARGIE   Someone new.

REES   Oh.

(*Exit* REES. MARGIE *sits.*)

MARGIE   God be in my head and in my heart and in my understanding.

(MARGIE *rises. Pause. Re-enter* REES.)

REES   (*over-casual, even hearty*) Well, now that really is rather—don't quite know what the word is?— coincidental. I suppose?

MARGIE   Who was it?

REES   Guy's friend Anthony.

MARGIE   Oh.

REES   He's coming down tomorrow. I said I wasn't
            sure there'd be much in the way of lunch it
            being a Monday but he said that didn't—

MARGIE   It's about Guy?

REES   He didn't say.

MARGIE   You didn't ask!

REES   Of course not.

MARGIE   Why not?

REES   My dear girl his tone made it clear he didn't
            wish to talk on the phone.

MARGIE   So you just agreed? Without knowing why he
            wants to see you?

REES   Well, naturally I'm sure it's something
            reasonably important—because, well, Anthony's
            hardly a frivolous person, is he?

MARGIE   Is he a spy too?

            (*Pause.*)

REES   Now, Margie—

MARGIE   Why not? He could be. He shared that flat with
            Guy during the war—you told me. That flat you
            took me to once where there were all those
            parties you didn't take me to just behind *Lilley
            and Skinners* in Oxford Street. And Anthony's
            other great friend apart from Guy is Queen
            Mary, isn't she? He tells her about art.

REES   He's certainly in charge of the royal art
            collection, yes.

MARGIE   Was it he who kept ringing?

REES   I didn't ask.

MARGIE   Oh. Well if the phone doesn't ring again we'll
            know it was, won't we? Now he's got you.

REES It needn't have been him. I wonder what he wants. You could be right—it could be about Guy.

MARGIE (*her hurt*) Oh, Rees—(*Pause. Dully:*) Well, perhaps we'd better go to bed? (*Pause.*) You don't want to tell me. (*Pause.*) You needn't.

REES I do want to.

(*Pause.*)

MARGIE I shan't ask again.

REES You won't?

MARGIE There is a limit to how many times.

REES Of course. (*He nods.*) Oh, Margie—I think Guy's gone to Moscow.

MARGIE Run away?

REES Mm. If I'm right—I need help. Your help.

MARGIE Oh, Rees, Rees.

(*Embrace.*)

REES Guy did ring to say goodbye. It all goes together now. Mind you, he denied it at the time.

MARGIE That Sunday—when he was full of that memo he'd written?

REES That was just flannel.

MARGIE You didn't tell me that, did you?

REES He swore me to silence, love.

MARGIE That's what you promised him—silence?

REES Yes. Yes. So I was forced to lie to you. He came back from America deliberately. To help a friend in the Foreign Office called Maclean.

MARGIE That man—?

REES Mm.

MARGIE (*as fact*) Who called you a rat.

REES	He was drunk.
MARGIE	Everyone heard. Everyone turned round.
REES	I was going to hit him.
MARGIE	You were too slow. He passed out.
REES	And we all laughed, Margie, didn't we?
MARGIE	It was still a pity you didn't hit him.
REES	I was too surprised.
MARGIE	He's a spy too, is he? What fun! Let's all laugh again. (*Hysteria gathers.*) What a hoot. A spy calls my husband a rat in public—we all laugh— again and again—
REES	Please! Margie! It isn't funny!
MARGIE	Don't you think so? I do—(*she doesn't*)
REES	Listen. (*Shakes her.*) Guy was ordered to help Maclean escape—he's under suspicion—I think Guy's gone with him. (*Painful giggles.*) Be sensible. Guy wouldn't have been meant to, I'm sure. His job was to look after Maclean, make sure Maclean didn't tell his wife who's expecting a baby any moment.
MARGIE	Guy'd be good at that.
REES	So now you know. (*Without conviction.*) Let's hope I'm wrong—
	(*Pause.*)
MARGIE	It's like before.
REES	When?
MARGIE	You say you want me to help you but you don't.
REES	I do.
MARGIE	But how can I? When you keep not telling me what matters?
REES	I have!

MARGIE	You haven't said why, have you? Still you haven't—why *did* Guy tell you he was a spy? At all? Why? In the first place?
REES	I did say, darling. To get it off his chest. (*Pause.*) You don't believe that?
MARGIE	Shall I tell you?
REES	I'm not sure guesses can be of much help—
MARGIE	(*overlap*) You're a spy too! You—Rees—you.
REES	(*explosive*) No! No—no no!
MARGIE	That Maclean man said you'd been one of them!
REES	He was wrong! I never was! I refused!
MARGIE	But Guy did ask you? Did try to make you one!
REES	Yes! Quite right. Yes. Yes, he did, yes, he did, yes. But that doesn't—
MARGIE	And that's why he told you he was—he'd have to, wouldn't he? If he wanted you to join?
REES	Not necessarily. It could've been just a confession.
MARGIE	Not with Guy! I said! I told you!
REES	Perhaps. Possibly. But I told Guy—not just when he tried to enrol me but several times after—I told him I wanted nothing, nothing to do with his clandestine activities. I told him I would not work for the Russian secret service. And we agreed to forget the whole thing. And we did—we wiped the slate clean.
MARGIE	But stayed friends?
REES	Don't sneer. It was on exactly that basis we could continue. That he could become Thomas's godfather—
MARGIE	I see.
REES	I hope so.

MARGIE   Except it doesn't seem all that clever of Guy to
            tell you he was going to help Maclean. I'd have
            thought he'd have kept that from you—that
            someone who'd refused to join in the first place
            would be the very last person he'd trust.

REES   It was as a friend. As a friend he did.

MARGIE   Spies can't have friends!

REES   Rubbish!

MARGIE   Can't be friends! Can't have them! Not here.
            Not in England—

REES   You're talking baloney!

MARGIE   I'm not! Oh, no! You wouldn't say that
            unless—you're still one aren't you? You must
            be—

REES   No! How many times? I refused! I never joined
            the Comintern. (*Pause—attempt at a laugh.*) Of
            course Guy being Guy he used to bitch
            sometimes—say no one ever refused, couldn't,
            one wasn't allowed to etcetera. I simply told him
            in that case I was the exception that proved the
            rule—

MARGIE   Oh, God—

REES   The living example of someone who had said
            no! (*He laughs.*) In the end we found we could
            laugh about it—there's always a funny side with
            Guy, don't forget.

MARGIE   But he went on insisting you'd said yes?

REES   No—not in any serious way, no—just a tease.

            (*Pause.*)

MARGIE   And Anthony? He said no too with a merry
            laugh?

REES   Irony doesn't suit you, Margie. It hardly ever
            sits well on a woman.

MARGIE   (*savage*) Lies don't suit you either!

REES   Margie—

MARGIE   Or do they? Perhaps they do?

REES   Don't let's—I shouldn't want to get angry. (*He drinks. Pause.*)

MARGIE   Tell me about Anthony. (*Pause.*) Oh my love. Can't you see how I wish, wish I didn't have to ask, didn't have to know? But I'm glad you did want my help—though I don't know if I can— I'll try to—if you'll let me. Except to help I've got to be told, haven't I? So I know what you know, so we can go on—together—with the children too, all of us—somehow. Somehow.

REES   Don't.

MARGIE   Because after all if Guy has done what you think then the police could come, couldn't they?—and the newspapers, and you'll have to answer all sorts of questions—me too I expect, but not so much—put by people who won't find what you say about old friends and before the war and Moscow being your holy city easy to understand. They won't care about you or us or anything. They'll just make what you call block judgements.

            (*Pause.*)

REES   When Guy asked me to join I said I had my doubts but if he could tell me who else had —

MARGIE   And he said Anthony?

REES   Promise you won't tell a soul! Guy swore me to secrecy—oh, bust it!

            (*Pause.*)

MARGIE   And that was that? Anthony's name did it?

REES   We all admired him. He was integrity personified.

MARGIE   So you did join?

REES   Not exactly—it just got accepted between
            us—oh, my love, I did warn when we first met
            that I was Mr Nobody.

MARGIE   You weren't, you were Major Rees, Royal
            Welch Fusiliers, and you looked wonderful. I
            asked you to marry me.

            (*Pause.*)

REES   And I did. And we've been happy, haven't we?
            Truly happy.

MARGIE   Yes. (*Pause.*) Have you stopped being a spy?

REES   Margie! I don't agree I ever was one. I've never
            stolen secrets. Never been in a position to know
            any! I've never been of use for the simple reason
            my career's never taken me into any of those
            jobs they want you to get—

MARGIE   Are you still a spy or not!?

REES   No! And as I see it I never was! All I did was
            say 'yes' for a while *en principe*! In principle.

MARGIE   How long is—in principle?

            (*Pause.*)

REES   Guy did want me to meet someone from the
            Soviet Embassy in London—a trade attaché, I
            believe—his and Anthony's case officer at the
            time as they're known—but I said no and when
            in 1939—you may not remember this—Stalin
            made that non-aggression treaty with Hitler—
            this answers your question, my darling—well,
            that did it for me. Once and for all. The scales
            fell from my eyes. Bonk. I told Guy then and
            there—he'd come tearing back from a holiday
            with Anthony at Monte Carlo to reassure
            us—the workers, the party faithful, as it were—I
            said, I told him, sorry, boy, that's it, for ever, if
            your precious Stalin can make a let's-be-friends
            pact with Hitler then we part company. Bang!
            And that's when we agreed to differ. Respect

each other, stand off from each other, be
different but remain friends.

MARGIE   Like Hitler and Stalin?

REES   You don't understand. (*Pause.*) Well, there you
            are. You've got it all now. I was asked, I didn't
            quite say no to begin with but I did in 1939.
            Long before I met you, my dear. That's all.

MARGIE   Until now?

REES   (*more sigh than word.*) Yes.

MARGIE   Guy still sees himself as your 'case' officer?

REES   Well, he's tried that on, yes, I agree.

MARGIE   But he's gone to Russia now?

REES   Well, we think so, don't we?

MARGIE   And that weekend? What did he really want?

REES   He wanted to be quite sure, absolutely sure, that
            whatever happened I wouldn't ever mention
            Anthony's name to anyone.

MARGIE   But you have—to me?

REES   Mm. By being honest I've made you—one of us
            you could say. Obviously Guy was at least
            considering going with Maclean even then.

            (*Pause.*)

MARGIE   Does he love Anthony?

REES   I think he did.

MARGIE   Not any more?

REES   No. These days I'd say he just appreciates how
            Anthony continues to love him.

MARGIE   Perhaps that can amount to the same thing?

REES   I don't think so. Of course they both still hang
            on to their old Cambridge ideals—especially of
            friendship.

            (*Pause.*)

MARGIE	And tomorrow? What will Anthony want tomorrow? More hush?
REES	I suppose so.
	(*Small pause.*)
MARGIE	So what are you going to do?
REES	Do?
MARGIE	Well, you can't just tell me, can you?
REES	Can't I?
MARGIE	No!
REES	Well, since Anthony is coming tomorrow—I must first—
MARGIE	No!
REES	Oh yes! I must talk to him first—yes! There's no question of that.
MARGIE	Why?
REES	Because he's a friend—a friend of Guy's.
MARGIE	But not of yours?
REES	Well—not especially but even—
MARGIE	No! He can't be! No! So why talk to him? No! You must ring him up. Now. Tell him you won't see him. This instant. After all.
REES	I can't do that!
MARGIE	You must, Rees, you must!
REES	No—
MARGIE	Can't you see you must?
REES	No—
MARGIE	Surely you can? Oh, Rees. Please. Say no. Please—say no.
	(*Pause.*)

Scene Two

Monday morning, 28th May—the following day.
ANTHONY, *in an elegant three-piece tweed suit, sits
perfectly still. After a moment* REES *enters with coffee on a
tray.*

REES   It's rather opportune—my wife taking the
            children into Reading.

ANTHONY   I like children.

REES   It means we can speak more freely. And in
            peace.

ANTHONY   Ah. Yes, I daresay.

            (REES *puts down the tray.*)

            Do I gather you're still convalescing?

REES   Not really. If I am it's self-indulgence. My
            doctor's given me the all clear. You always take
            your coffee black I seem to remember?

ANTHONY   No. Not any more. White-ish nowadays. Less
            acid. No sugar though. I hope it hasn't put you
            about—my coming down?

REES   No—you said on the phone you'd prefer it.

ANTHONY   Your wife didn't mind either? I should hate to—

REES   Oh, no. No. She drives the two eldest into
            school anyway and she had some shopping—
            there you are. (*He hands the coffee.*) It's the
            powdered variety.

ANTHONY   I drink anything. (*Sips it.*) Perfect. Am I to
            understand Guy telephoned your wife last
            Friday morning while you were in Oxford?

            (*Pause.*)

REES   I imagine Jimmy told you that? He phoned
            Margie too.

ANTHONY   Yes, that's right. Guy's never been discreet and
            your wife would have had no reason to be. Not

on Saturday. After all you hadn't got back by
then, had you?

REES   You appear fully appraised of my recent
            movements.

ANTHONY   Jimmy again.

REES   What made him think Guy might've come here?

ANTHONY   Don't know. Bow at a venture? Jimmy rang
            everywhere—he seems to have panicked. But
            he's fine now. I read the riot act to him, the
            silly boy. What exactly did he say to your wife?
            Did she tell you?

REES   I really do think you ought to put me in the
            picture first. About yourself.

ANTHONY   Oh? I've been assuming you were already *au
            fait*? That Guy had told all as usual?

            (REES *chooses not to reply. Pause.*)

            How did Guy seem—to your wife when he
            phoned?

REES   Garbled.

ANTHONY   Drunk?

REES   She thought it likely. Or on pills. He didn't
            want to speak to me personally, he said, well,
            not to start with, he changed his mind later on,
            said he'd go to Oxford but he didn't—in the
            event.

ANTHONY   One could wish he had.

REES   He said he'd just rung to say—well, it was more
            or less goodbye, I suppose?

            (*Pause.*)

ANTHONY   He didn't even say that to me.

REES   He told you nothing?

ANTHONY   Yes.

REES	I'm sorry. It seems unfair—though logical if he were going to—
ANTHONY	I'm not sure we've time to be mawkish. What else did he say—garbled or otherwise?
REES	According to my wife he said—
ANTHONY	Do you doubt her?
REES	No. Figure of speech.
ANTHONY	Ah.
REES	According to her he said I'd understand what it was he was about to do—
ANTHONY	Do you?
REES	I had an inkling. But he was very vague at Margie—although he did emphasize to her that I must not forget that we were friends— whatever happened he and I were friends.
ANTHONY	Guy's always set great store by his friendships. I don't mean his casual liaisons, of course. His real friendships.
REES	I know. (*Steel.*) He could get very tedious about it. Quote Morgan Forster *ad nauseam*.
ANTHONY	Quite. It was his creed. Mine too. Still is.
REES	Really? I find Forster's friend versus country argument charming but deceptive.
ANTHONY	Morgan is a charmer. You said you had some notion of what Guy was talking about?
REES	Yes.
ANTHONY	You don't have to be on the defensive about Guy to me.
REES	I'm not.
ANTHONY	He came to see you, didn't he? The moment he got back from America?

REES	No, he went to see you first at the Courtauld— or so he said—then caught the morning train here. Did he do that?
ANTHONY	Yes. Yes, he did. Quite right. He came to see me, yes. Did he tell you why he'd come back?
REES	I got a lot of FO flannel first. Never has that particular abbreviation seemed so appropriate.
ANTHONY	(*icy smile*) Guy always insisted you had a sense of humour. Anyway, in the end he confided in you?
REES	Yes. But how completely or reliably I'd hesitate to say. He certainly suggested you'd been instrumental in arranging his recall from the USA—although ostensibly it was for a driving offence.
ANTHONY	Quite right, I was. Did he add to that?
REES	Yes.
ANTHONY	Do say—for all our sakes.
REES	Has Guy gone too?

(*Pause.*)

ANTHONY	It's still rather early to say—
REES	But it looks like it?
ANTHONY	Yes.
REES	We'd hardly be meeting otherwise.
ANTHONY	No. I suspect I'm more in the dark than you are.
REES	Really? Guy said you were in overall charge?
ANTHONY	How grand that sounds. No—rather more like a Cook's tour operator.
REES	Who's lost one of his charges?
ANTHONY	If you like. Guy was simply meant to ensure that Maclean got clear. Nothing else. *Aller et retour.* Go—come back.

REES	As far as Paris or as far as Berne?
ANTHONY	(*inbreath*) He gave you the itinerary?
REES	Mm. I made it the price of my silence.
ANTHONY	I see.
REES	To be fully informed.
ANTHONY	When did he tell you all this?
REES	That same weekend. Well, on the Monday—we travelled up to town together. What he didn't say, however, was that he was seriously contemplating going himself.
ANTHONY	I see.
REES	So I consider I still have a certain freedom of choice.
ANTHONY	You do?
REES	Mm. I asked him directly but he denied it. He said it would break your heart if he went too.
ANTHONY	(*cover*) Guy often over-states. He was supposed to phone me from Paris on Saturday evening.
REES	Perhaps he will from Berne?
ANTHONY	Guy's orders were to accompany Donald only as far as Paris. Someone else was to take over— there.
REES	None of you trust Maclean, it would seem?
ANTHONY	Not at all, we do. But it's awfully difficult to make the complete break required in a situation like this. Imagine it for yourself. For anyone. Leaving wives or friends behind. Without a word. We're all human. Any of us might have second thoughts.
REES	And after Berne? Guy suggested Prague to me.
ANTHONY	(*nod*) There's a trade fair. Donald was to get a visa in Berne for Prague. Guy would have no difficulty in getting one as well. They'll be

handing them out like lollipops. After all they're both still—if that's where they are—bona fide British diplomatists.

REES   Once in Prague they'll go to the Soviet Embassy?

ANTHONY   Those were Donald's instructions.

REES   But now they're getting two for the price of one.

ANTHONY   (*wan smile*) They may not be entirely pleased.

REES   So what are you going to do?

ANTHONY   No—no. The question is what are you going to do? Or rather first—what have you already done?

REES   Nothing. I only got back from Oxford last night—after all.

ANTHONY   I see. Fortunately no one's alerted the newspapers.

REES   Are you suggesting I might?

ANTHONY   Of course not, no.

REES   I daresay Jimmy could. Or whoever else he phoned apart from Margie.

ANTHONY   Not now. I've plugged those loopholes. I had quite a busy time on Saturday and Sunday— tidying up Guy's flat—sorting out his effects— getting in touch with everyone Jimmy'd got in touch with. Fortunately Guy's reputation can explain almost anything.

REES   So you reckon you've made everything as watertight as you can except for me—is that right?

ANTHONY   Yes. As I see it Guy's delivered me to you as a sort of farewell present bound hand and foot.

REES   Hardly—surely?

ANTHONY   Together with someone else, I suspect? Did he speak to you of his time in America?

REES	Profusely. He explained about Philby and the FBI and the CIA's new chief—Maclean's unauthorized pass—and his cryptonym of 'Homer'—everything.
ANTHONY	Obviously Guy thought you worthy of the highest trust?
REES	(*grin*) No. Even before I demanded to be fully informed he knew he was in a weak position. After all he'd come to beg me to keep quiet on your behalf—he loves you in his way, I'm sure.
	(*Pause*)
ANTHONY	To recapitulate for a moment—you genuinely feel you still have freedom of choice?
REES	(*ice*) Yes.
ANTHONY	To speak your mind as it were?
REES	Yes.
ANTHONY	I'm surprised but I'm sure we can come back to that—next, I wonder if you'd agree that—dare I say it?—that a conventionally married man is rarely if ever entirely his own master? (*Pause.*) I mean that purely factually not offensively, of course.
REES	Of course. I'd agree that if he loves his wife she will mean more to him than any friend ever can.
	(*Pause.*)
ANTHONY	(*blurt*) In that case what have you told her?
	(*Pause.*)
REES	She'd been upset by a number of phone calls—I don't mean Guy's or Jimmy's—but yours—I'm pretty sure they emanated from you—
ANTHONY	I did try several times, I admit. I apologize. When your wife answered I couldn't bring myself to speak. I was so concerned, even rather jittery—as I hope you can understand?
REES	You spoke to her the last time.

ANTHONY	Yes—I'd calmed down by then. I'm sorry.
REES	They disturbed her dreadfully. She said they made her feel she was being drawn into a conspiracy which might be criminal. I saw her point.

(*Pause.*)

ANTHONY	May I be frank?
REES	Only you can answer that.
ANTHONY	(*snap*) I can't say I've ever been entirely convinced of your loyalty. I warned Guy about you many times.
REES	I'm sure you did. But I have been loyal to date.
ANTHONY	I must disagree.
REES	Why?
ANTHONY	You had a word with a friend of a friend last night, I believe?
REES	(*very still*) Who told you that?
ANTHONY	You asked to be put in touch with someone in MI5 whom we both happen to know actually.
REES	Who?
ANTHONY	Guy's namesake. Guy Liddell. He's second in command now.
REES	(*sigh*) I ought to have guessed.
ANTHONY	I imagine your wife pushed you into it?
REES	I simply asked one of the few people I happen to know in your world if I might have a general chat later on this week.
ANTHONY	Nothing specific?
REES	What I said—a general chat. It was—yes— partly to keep Margie happy—yes. She felt strongly I ought to do something. Report my suspicions and so on. To begin with I refused,

said I needed to talk to you before anything else
but unfortunately she'd been so alarmed by your
phone calls she wouldn't be satisfied with that.

ANTHONY I brought it on myself?

REES Up to a point, certainly. However I took care to
be entirely noncommital.

ANTHONY You can be quite sure you gave no indication at
all—even inadvertently—of what we assume has
happened?·

REES I know I didn't. And if I'm as frank as you
hope to be then I did it to calm Margie down so
I could get a night's sleep in order to be fit to
face you. (*Pause.*) I'm sure you appreciate my
position?

ANTHONY As you do mine, I trust.

REES I happen to know a great deal I now find I'd
rather not know but which others should know.

ANTHONY But against that you have certain old loyalties.

REES Of course. But then again there's my wife. Even
my children.

ANTHONY Guy's godfather to one of them, isn't he?

REES Yes. Not that that cuts much ice with Margie.

ANTHONY She dislikes him?

REES Only in some aspects. But if he's gone to
Moscow most of our feelings become irrelevant,
anyway—wouldn't you say?

ANTHONY Probably.

REES We none of us need waste time any more liking
or disliking him.

ANTHONY I daresay not.

REES In effect it'll be as if he's died?

(ANTHONY *does not reply—he moves away from*
REES.)

As I see it once someone's done something as
irrevocable as that those left behind are free to
examine their own consciences and act
accordingly.

ANTHONY   I'd have thought there was more at stake than
any one person's interpretation of his own
integrity?

REES   That's party doctrine?

ANTHONY   Is it? I don't bother with the ideological side any
more. Rather arid—

REES   Too many angels perched on too many
pinpricks?

ANTHONY   It is a religion for some, I agree. As for me I
find increasingly the Courtauld and the Royal
Collection occupy all my time. Were you given
an appointment for your chat?

REES   No, they'd be in touch, I was told.

ANTHONY   Quite. I always maintained you might turn out
to be our Achilles' heel—in this country at any
rate. Guy always disagreed—he insisted despite
all your doubts—some might say vacillations—
he was sure you had what he called 'the heart of
the matter' in you. He is a generous soul, mind
you. He used to say that apart from me you
were his oldest friend and in the last event we
could trust you. Can you really contemplate
betraying him?

REES   If he's gone he's done that for me.

ANTHONY   But as we don't know for certain—?

REES   Then no! Not easily, no. Of course not—I'd
have thought that was obvious. But one could
look at it the other way round—that he's
betrayed me and you, come to that. Perhaps as
you say we ought not to be too sentimental?

ANTHONY   You've made up your mind?

REES	Pretty well.
ANTHONY	Thanks to your wife?
REES	She's helped—yes.
	(*Pause.*)
ANTHONY	Suppose you're wrong? Suppose you were to speak out and then Guy were to come back with a perfectly genuine reason for his absence? Your allegations unsupported by admissible evidence wouldn't be enough to bring him to trial—they would however have besmirched your oldest friend for life. At the least surely you should wait?
REES	Give him time to get away?
ANTHONY	Give him time to declare himself by his own actions.
REES	(*almost speechless*) You—speak as if—as if we didn't both know what Guy is! What you are! What Maclean is and Philby is—
ANTHONY	And you, Rees, you!
REES	(*total anger released at last*) No! For the last time, no! Get your bloody hooks out of me! And take yourself out of my garden while you're about it! Go on!
ANTHONY	I think you should reflect a little longer. Having worked in MI5 I can guarantee we—I'm sorry—they—though one never really retires from any secret service—they won't take your own account of yourself on your simple say so—sincerely put though I'm sure it would be. They'll assume you've got reasons for speaking against your erstwhile friends which have very little to do with your own stated probity or patriotism.
REES	I shall have to tell them the truth! That I renounced my youthful commitment to the International back in '39—that the Molotov-

Ribbentrop pact finally opened my eyes to the *realpolitik* of Stalin—

ANTHONY   I'm talking of ours. Our *realpolitik*. For instance I'm certain they'll wonder why it's taken you so long to confess your complicity—

REES   It wasn't. I've just said—

ANTHONY   It's going to look awfully odd—why have you waited a dozen years? Why? And that thought could cause them to ponder your war—your service years. And they'll find, if they don't already know it by then, that as a staff officer with General Montgomery no less you were privy, I recall, to the detailed planning of D-Day—

REES   I shall have to risk all that—I don't suppose it will be particularly pleasant.

ANTHONY   I can assure you it won't be. They'll see your renunciation of the Comintern as just a routine smokescreen for what you really did in the war.

            (*Pause.*)

REES   You'll discredit me before I even get there?

ANTHONY   Not at all. I'm the beggar at your table.

REES   Trying to saw the legs off undetected?

ANTHONY   (*laughing*) You've always talked well. All I'm suggesting is that you might extend your loyalty from Guy to me—if only as a *memento mori* of your past ideals. When they do get in touch you can always say what seemed important last night—no longer seems so today. Mm?

REES   I wish that were true—though I don't expect you to believe me.

ANTHONY   Perhaps I can? Perhaps rather more easily than Guy or Donald or Kim? I can even respect up to a point those scruples you felt in 1939. It was a difficult moment for me, too, I found,

                   although I managed to reconcile Stalin's
                   approach with my hopes for socialism's final
                   victory in a way you say you couldn't.

REES   Perhaps holidaying in the South of France
                   helped?

ANTHONY   (*humourless*) I shouldn't've thought so. And my
                   faith was justified in fact—

REES   When Russia entered the war on our side
                   against fascism?

ANTHONY   Yes. Stalin redeemed himself in our eyes at that
                   moment. I always thought you might come back
                   to us then—so did Guy. We lived in hope—told
                   ourselves you might. You came to so many of
                   our parties, seemed so glad to be with us. Of
                   course we were all over the moon—it did seem
                   to be the turning point—there we were—the
                   people of Britain shoulder to shoulder with the
                   people of Russia—do you remember how we all
                   queued in the rain for hours just to glimpse the
                   Stalingrad sword?

REES   No. As I remember, Guy sent relays of able
                   seamen to queue for you.

ANTHONY   Nonsense. One of his tall stories. We found it
                   really was bliss to be alive.

REES   History had proved faithful to you in her
                   fashion?

ANTHONY   Certainly we, who, like you, might have
                   capitulated to nihilism and cynicism, had been
                   spared that fate. With clear consciences we could
                   now help our Russian allies as much as we'd
                   always wanted to.

REES   And doubtless you did?

ANTHONY   What a pity you'd reneged and could only think
                   in crabby Churchillian terms of Russia as a
                   friend of mere convenience?

REES   Even if I were to do what you want and
            wait—once the news is out the security services
            are going to remember I got in touch, then put
            them off, aren't they?

ANTHONY   Oh, yes, they'll come back to you, of course.
            But by then we could be in a stronger position—
            I'd be pleased to advise you.

REES   Yes, I'm sure!

ANTHONY   (*unruffled*) The sin of omission is usually
            effective. Simply not say or not know. Wish one
            did.

REES   They can be put off as easily as that?

ANTHONY   They could be rather tougher with you. They
            aren't going to condemn anyone out of hand.
            Least of all someone like myself—not on one
            disaffected ex-agent's word. (*Pause.*) And look
            what happened to Walter Krivitsky.

REES   Guy once mentioned him.

ANTHONY   I'm not surprised. A cautionary tale. Yes. He
            betrayed his friends in the International—even
            tried to impugn Donald and Kim—fortunately
            his evidence was unsubstantive—did Guy tell
            you how Krivitsky died?

REES   No.

ANTHONY   In unresolved circumstances. There was a
            suicide note of no particular conviction.

REES   He was murdered?

ANTHONY   One might hazard that small guess.

REES   Why mention it?

ANTHONY   Just so—just so you don't reject my offer of help
            out of hand. I can brief you. You'd go fore-
            armed. Our people are traditionalist,
            unimaginative but that doesn't mean they're
            negligible except in the inevitable historical
            sense—in that context, of course, they're as easy

to deceive as one's dear old nanny. As a friend
I'd be happy to help. I'm uniquely qualified to
do so, of course.

(*Pause.*)

REES   (*very still*) Of course.

ANTHONY   I shall miss Guy—so much. As I'm sure you
will?

REES   I wonder? I might find I feel a sense of relief.
Perhaps you should go too? Join him?

ANTHONY   (*icy*) Is that a joke?

REES   No, a thought. It seems logical to me.

ANTHONY   Leave you to have a field day?

REES   (*grin*) I daresay I'll have one anyway.

ANTHONY   Is that your final word?

REES   Not quite. I never want to see or hear from you
again. Or from Guy. I intend to tell the
authorities what I believe is appropriate without
your connivance or prompting—

ANTHONY   You over-simplify—

REES   By God I don't! I shall tell them everything I
know! I've got nothing to hide, nothing to be
ashamed of except remaining silent, remaining
loyal to a friend, for far too long—fifteen years
too long! Yes, that was foolish but being a fool
and being deceived—because Guy's deceived me
just as much as he's deceived you and that I
don't forgive—you may, I don't—but as I say—
being a fool is not as bad as being a traitor—

ANTHONY   I warn you, Rees! Betray us, you'll betray
yourself.

REES   No! That doesn't wash any more! You can't stir
my conscience that way! To hell with you. Go
on—go to Moscow and get yourself a British
Railway sandwich on the train—you'll just catch
the twelve twenty one. Go on—out of here—

ANTHONY	Celtic rhetoric aside, Rees—
REES	Out!
ANTHONY	— I don't believe you of all people now accept a notion as outmoded as my country right or wrong? Our fathers died for that nonsense in 1914—
REES	Blast your history—get out of my garden!
ANTHONY	And however much you tell yourself you no longer agree with Morgan Forster it isn't that easy to dismiss him either—
REES	But it is! Especially with what you've all made of it! Go on—say it! Say it! If I—(*He grasps* ANTHONY's *lapel.*)
ANTHONY	Let go! Please. This is too absurd—why should I—?
REES	No! Say it! Like Guy used to. Your party piece. Go on! If I had to choose—
ANTHONY	Oh, really! No, Rees, there's no need.
REES	After me! If I had to choose—Go on!
	(*Pause.*)
ANTHONY	If I had to choose—
REES	Between betraying my country—
ANTHONY	Between betraying my country—So childish!
REES	And betraying my friend I hope—Go on.
ANTHONY	And betraying my friend I hope—
REES	I'd have the guts to betray my country.
ANTHONY	I'd have the guts—(*He stops.*)
REES	Say it or choke on it!
ANTHONY	To what purpose?
REES	So I hear you!
ANTHONY	(*crack*)—to betray my country.

REES	And the phrase you always left out? So conveniently? How did that go? How does he preface it? How?
ANTHONY	What do you mean? What?
REES	You don't remember? You must! Go on!
ANTHONY	No! Please. This is—what can it possibly do or prove?
REES	He said 'I hate the idea of causes'—so do I—
ANTHONY	Morgan meant—
REES	I know what he meant! It isn't he just hates bone-headed patriots—he detests boss-eyed Utopians too. His trust is in the person entirely—in his friend. Nothing else. As you know perfectly well but that hasn't stopped you stealing what he said, has it? Twisting it! Using it as camouflage—sheeps's clothing—while you sabotage everything you pretend to honour—
ANTHONY	Not so! You simply can't say that—
REES	Why not? I just have! But what Forster failed to mention is our friends are our country just as much as this ground we stand on! And our wives are also our friends as are our children too and the whole human ragbagful is us, is England in all its, our, interwoven, unique, infinitely valuable individual complexities. And as such we don't care to be thought of as raw material for your art of history! Now get out of my garden!

(*He pushes* ANTHONY *backwards dismissively but* ANTHONY *trips and falls awkwardly. He lies still.*)

(*Alarm.*) Oh, no! I didn't mean—oh, Lord. (*He bends over* ANTHONY.) Anthony—are you all right?

(*Enter* MARGIE.)

MARGIE	Rees! I heard you shouting— Oh no! What have you done?
REES	Margie! I was just telling him to go—

MARGIE   It sounded much worse than that—

REES   He tripped.

            (ANTHONY *moans, groans.*)

MARGIE   Is he all right. Mr Blunt—?

ANTHONY   (*sitting up*) Blacked out. For a moment.

REES   I'm sorry.

ANTHONY   So am I. (*He shakes his head.*) Most untoward.
            (*He starts to get up.*)

MARGIE   Don't get up too soon.

REES   No, take your time.

ANTHONY   (*curt*) I'm fine! It wasn't anything. Nothing at
            all. (*He rises, brushes himself down.*)

REES   I apologize.

ANTHONY   I shouldn't—it might suggest you hadn't meant
            it. Good day, Mrs Rees, I was just about to go
            when you arrived—if anything it was your
            husband who detained me.

MARGIE   Any news of Guy?

ANTHONY   It appeared at first we had a great deal to
            discuss but in the end we hadn't. (*To* REES.)
            I'll do my best to make sure you're let down as
            lightly as possible. Not only for your sake but
            for your wife and children, too.

            (*And on this warning note he goes. Pause.*)

MARGIE   What's he going to do?

REES   Aren't you back rather soon? I thought you'd—

MARGIE   I was worried. What did he mean?

REES   You were afraid I'd go back on my word?

            (*Pause.*)

MARGIE   Mm.

REES   Fair enough—but I didn't.

MARGIE	Oh, Rees.
REES	He tried to threaten me—said if I told the authorities he'd drag me through the mud —
MARGIE	Well, you must act first!
REES	Let's hope they believe me—he's one of them too, Margie.
MARGIE	All the more reason for speaking out straight-away! You're doing the right thing, Rees! Really!
REES	So why do I feel so bloody awful?
MARGIE	Oh, Rees! You've got to believe in yourself!
REES	Yes, I've always told myself that—
MARGIE	I can't manage if you don't!
REES	I do really but in such a lop-sided, cack-handed way. Always whistled to keep whoever I was warm in the dark. No self. No sense of self at all—
MARGIE	You mustn't be little boy lost—not anymore—
REES	And when I do make a stand, state my case for what it's worth—look what happens—people faint on me—absurd!
MARGIE	But that doesn't matter, does it? Not if you're right?
REES	Things aren't as simple as that, love. Never ever.
MARGIE	Perhaps they should be?
REES	A fond hope.
MARGIE	All right! But I prefer that to—to nothing at all.
REES	Oh, my dear. I'll try, yes I will, to get an idea of myself. Get it from somewhere or other. Somehow.
MARGIE	Do you mean that?
	(*Pause.*)

REES   Mm. Meanwhile I'll do what I can. Tell MI5
what I know. But I bet I'm the one who's left
feeling he's the traitor. I'll ring them now.

(*He goes.* MARGIE *stands alone.*)

END

PROPERTY LIST

FURNITURE

2 wicker chairs (with cushions on seats)
Round low wicker coffee table
Square wicker occasional table
Wicker chaise longue/day bed (no arms/with cushions on seats and back)

ACT ONE

Very thick Foreign Office memorandum (stoutly bound)
Bottle of Bell's Whisky
Soda syphon with wicker cover
2 whisky tumblers — Crystal
Wicker tray (To hold: Whisky bottle, Soda syphon & Whisky tumblers)
Cigarettes (Guy) — Camel untipped
Zippo lighter (Guy)
Golliwog
Wooden train
Fire Engine
Teddy Bear
Wooden Rocking Horse
Bottle of Chablis
2 Crystal wine glasses
Wooden tray (To hold: Chablis bottle & two glasses)
3 ashtrays
Cigarettes (Rees) — Players Navy Cut
Lighter (Rees)

ACT TWO, Scene One

Cowboy suit & hat — Flash American
Toy gun belt & gun
Candle lamp — has to burn for 45 minutes
Picture Post (May 1951)
Bottle of Bell's Whisky
2 Whisky tumblers (Same as Act 1)
Soda Syphon (Same as Act 1)
Tray for Whisky etc. (Same as Act 1)
2 ashtrays (Same as Act 1)

Briefcase — stuffed full of papers
Matches
Cigarettes (Rees)
Lighter (Rees)

ACT TWO, Scene Two

Coffee Pot
2 Coffee Cups & Saucers
Cream Jug
Sugar Bowl
Tray (for above)
2 Ashtrays (Same as Act 1)
Cigarettes (Rees)
Lighter (Rees)

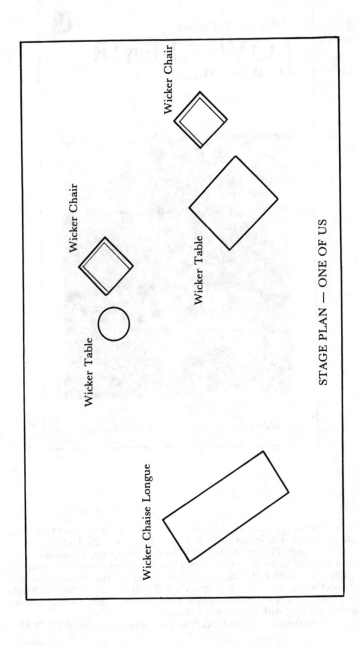

Wicker Chair

Wicker Chair

Wicker Table

Wicker Table

Wicker Chaise Longue

STAGE PLAN — ONE OF US

LOVE AFFAIR
ALFRED SHAUGHNESSY

adapted from 'Coup de Soleil' by Marcel Mithois

A deliciously light and very funny version of the highly successful Paris comedy *Coup de Soleil* set in Paris in the spring of 1925. During a recent UK tour, Sian Phillips starred as Valentine Matignon, a passionate and vivacious lady in her 40s who becomes bored with her regular lover and falls madly in love with a dashing young florist. When her son returns home with an older woman he wishes to marry, she is clearly not in approval but hardly in a position to criticise. Sparkling dialogue and excellent characterisations invest this play with a great sense of style.

For further details contact, ETG, 129 Park Street, London W1Y 3FA.

THERESE RAQUIN
LESLIE SANDS

a stage adaptation of Emile Zola's novel

A skilful adaptation of the 19th Century novel with a special twist to Zola's original ending. This well-paced and gripping tale of retribution provides a penetrating study of sexual obsession and guilt. The play tells the story of the secret affair between Thérèse Raquin and her husband's best friend, Laurent, and reveals the strength of the passion which incites them to murder. The murder, however, leads to neither happiness nor liberation, but to the destruction of their relationship and their eventual downfall. 'Plunging straight into the passionate relationship between Thérèse and the artist, Laurent, (the play) compresses the carefully constructed preamble to the central crime...(the couple) pass from a stimulating clandestine indulgence through a chilling climax to the wastes of destructive circumspection.' *Daily Telegraph.*
For further details contact, ETG, 129 Park Street, London W1Y 3FA.